THIS BOOK BELONGS TO

Find 2 Differences

Following The Dashed Line
And Color The Picture After Finish

Color By Number

1: Light Brown   3: Skin Color   5: Red   7: Violet   9: White

2: Sky Blue   4: Yellow   6: Orange   8: Green

Find The Correct Shadow

Help The Dog Get Home

Find 4 Hidden Objects In This Picture

How To Draw A Dog Face

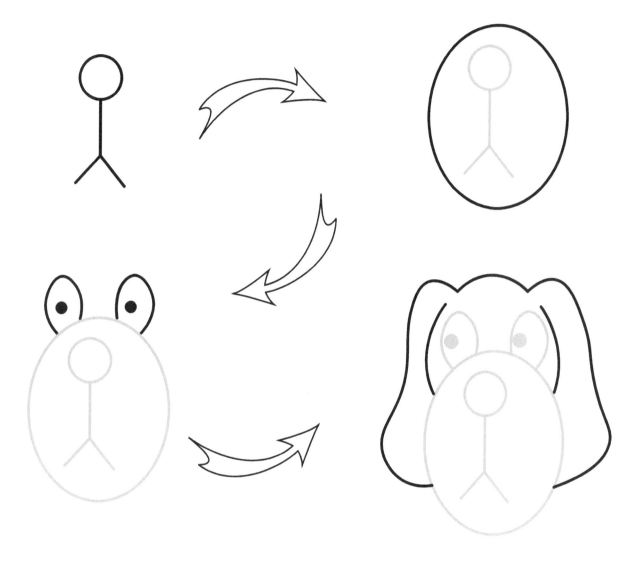

PRACTICE

Made in United States
Troutdale, OR
12/17/2023

15966511R00058